HEART AND SOUL

HEART AND SOUL

Francisco Cândido Xavier

Emmanuel – Spirit

Heart and Soul
Translation copyright © 2017 by
United States Spiritist Council (Jussara Korngold)

All rights reserved. No part of this publication may be reproduced, stored in or introduced into a retrieval system, or transmitted, in any form, or by any means (electronic, mechanical, photocopying, recording or otherwise) without the prior written permission of the publisher, except in the case of brief quotations and if the source and publisher are mentioned.
United States Spiritist Council
http://www.spiritit.us
Email: info@spiritist.us
Original Title: Alma e Coração – FRANCISCO CÂNDIDO XAVIER/Emmanuel

ISBN: 0998648140
ISBN: 9780998648149
Library of Congress Control Number: 2017941380
United States Spiritist Council

Translation: Publio Lentulus Vicente Coelho
Editing: Marcia Andrade and Jussara Korngold (2017)

Cover design: Mauro de Souza Rodrigues

Main entry under title:
Heart and Soul
1. Religious Philosophy 2. Spiritist Doctrine 3. Christianity I. Xavier, Francisco C. /Emmanuel
Manufactured in the United States of America

Index

    Preface. ix
    Heart and Soul xi

1. Starting Again 1
2. You will Love by Serving 3
3. Environments. 5
4. A Step Up 7
5. A Donation from the Heart 9
6. Giving 11
7. Your Place 13
8. In Life's Account 15
9. Before the Law of Good 17
10. Personal Environment 19
11. Your Mind 21
12. Towards the Kingdom of God. 23
13. From Sunrise to Sunset 25
14. Trials of Beloved Ones 27
15. You will follow the Light 29
16. The Effect of Forgiveness 33
17. Hidden Heroism 35
18. Between God and the Neighbor. 37

19	Firmness and Gentleness	39
20	Above us	41
21	Disturbances and Obsession	43
22	You will be Patient	45
23	Ideals and Action	47
24	Forgiveness in the Familiar Environment	49
25	Divine Seeds	51
26	Attacks on Good Works	53
27	Difficult Companions	55
28	Judgments	57
29	Emotional Disturbances	59
30	Fortune	61
31	Other Enemies	63
32	Speaking and Listening	65
33	Beloved Family	67
34	Spiritual Support	69
35	Your Possessions	71
36	In Matters of Faith	73
37	Peace of Mind	75
38	Reactions	77
39	You will Help for Love	79
40	Our Problems	81
41	Indication of Life	83
42	Before the Fallen	85
43	Near You	87
44	Conversation in Family	89
45	Mutual Support	91
46	Moral Assistance	93
47	Offenses and Offenders	95
48	Trials and Prayers	97
49	Giving and Doing	99

50 How to Forgive 101
51 We are not Exceptions 103
52 Opponents 105
53 Arguments.. 107
54 In the Sublime Initiation 109
55 Our Share 111
56 God Shall Come 113
57 The Best Happens................................ 115
58 Service to those who Serve...................... 117
59 About Virtue 119
60 Trust in God..................................... 121

Preface

At this time, in which many peoples have their peace disturbed, and countless households are struggling, disarranging, and dissolving, aggravating the sufferings of humanity, the world is more than ever needed and eager for a solace. It needs a light that springs from the heart and soul, and no more from the cold and hazy brain.

Thus, the opportunity of this book, whose title matches very well with its context, so mild and cozy, that it seems to us a flowery and smiley meadow, open to the tired traveler, who searches for hours of rest and reflection.

Its lines have flown from the pen of someone who, having made of the healthy Spiritualism his most sacred priesthood, has devoted his entire life to ease the moral and physical pain of the neighbor, both in his acts and words. This is because he is not a simple theoretical, but a constantly active practitioner of the good.

Hence, the reader will find in this book an encouraging message, distributed in sixty short and well-concatenated chapters on varied topics, all converging such as streams of light to the same ocean of Truth, who is God, and quenching the thirst of the pilgrim souls from all backgrounds.

In each chapter, the reader will have a theme for meditation. If he meditates on each of them, and practices it until the end, he will be able to build a happy world within himself, which will help him to come a bit closer to the source of the so dreamed and decanted happiness; indeed, really fetched by so few.

By publishing this work, we believe to be contributing to its message about the purpose of reaching all souls, enlightening their hearts and harmonizing their minds, thus leading them to tread nobly the path of spirituality, the unique able to relieve the bitterness of life, and take them to the "Kingdom of God", which is more inside than outside each one of us.

We wish to confirm and materialize our beliefs so that both the author and the publishers feel compensated in their intent and effort.

The Publishers.

Heart and Soul

Here, we present to the dear reader, a brief introduction to the pages of this book.

They do not result from constant researches in important libraries, as they were born from the fountain of experience.

Together, under the light of prayer, the incarnated fellows and us, the friends living in the Beyond, have written such pages within the course of reflections and debates about the millennial problems, of the being and the destiny, the search and suffering.

After emphasizing this or that topic of the Spiritist Doctrine, which brings to us again the Gospel of Jesus, we have exchanged ideas and comments on the fundamental and simple truths of the Universe; therefore, they are fragments of love, gathered from fraternal dialogues, in the attempt of adjusting ourselves to the realities of the Spirit.

Generous interlocutors often came to visit and honor us with their word and attention. Not only came them from laureate circles of academic achievements, but also from the laborious centers of practical life; not only from the serious duties of the household but also from the tortured regions of adversities and ordeals that improve existence.

Many others, for goodness, brought their spirit full of anxiety and tears, or tormented by pain; hungry for hope and thirsty for God.

As we were assembled with the single goal of searching for spiritual progress, we exchanged the innermost thoughts in friendly meetings, from which this modest book was born in our revitalizing harvest of faith.

Therefore, forgive us, if we dedicate to you a simple book, as simple as our possibilities of expression. Nevertheless, believe this book is all intertwined with threads of soul and heart, in the vows we make to the Lord, to illuminate and bless us all so that tomorrow we are able to offer something better and more fruitful.

Emmanuel
Uberaba, July 26th, 1969

1

Starting Again

So many mistakes, sadness, tears, and chronic imbalance…
Sometimes you believe that all the blessings are extinct, and all the doors are closed to the required invigoration…

You forget, though, that the wisdom of life determines that every morning brings a new day.

Starting again is the process of Nature, from the simple seeds to the solar giant.

If you have felt the weight of disillusionment, then nothing obliges you to remain in the situation of disenchantment. Resume the construction of your ideals on a stronger basis and go back to the warmth of experience, in order to cultivate them in the fullness of new forces.

If failure has visited you in the endeavor for elevation, this is no reason for regret and self-pity, once the frustration of the expectations often means an order from the Almighty to change routes, and starting once more is the path to the desired triumph.

Perhaps we have been careless before others, cultivating indifference or ingratitude; nevertheless, it is perfectly possible to amend attitudes and restart the planting of sympathy by offering kindness and comprehension to those surrounding us.

We have lost affections that we assumed steadfast; though, it is not fair to fall into despair for it. Time allows us to start again in search of the real affinities; those susceptible to give us the courage to bear the trials of the path and ensure us the joy of living.

Let us get rid of bitter thoughts, feelings of anguish, resentments, and sorrows back to the heart. Let us open the windows of the soul, in order that the Sun of understanding may clean and reheat our inner house.

Everything in life can start one more time, so as to fulfill the law of growth and development in all directions.

In fact, on many occasions when we neglect the opportunities and tasks that we have been granted in the Work of the Lord, we will return later to experience and be responsible for them again, but it will never be too late.

2

You will Love by Serving

You will love, by serving.

Even when you hear allusions about the supposed decline of human values, extolling the forces of darkness, you will make of your own soul a glow to light the path.

Even when ambition and pride come by surprise with suspicions and resentments, you will love, by serving, always.

When someone points out the evils of the world, you shall remember those people who supported your feebleness of childhood, and those who helped you to pronounce the first prayer. You shall remember those who encouraged your ideals of good in the birthplace; and those who left the Earth, blessing your name after repeated examples of sacrifice, so you could live freely.

You will remember the anonymous benefactors, who gave you understanding and hope while faithful to the apostolate of love and service that they bequeathed to you...

Therefore, you will not remain at the surface of words, but you will put yourself in the place of those who suffer, so you do to them everything you wish they did to you, under the same circumstances.

Before the victims of poverty, think what would be of you, in the refuges of nobody, in the night cold, carrying the body exhausted and sore, to which the begged bread did not provide enough sustenance…

When close to helpless patients, reflect on how would be the abandonment under the weight of illness, without even the presence of a friend to alleviate the burden of sorrow…

Before the children thrown on the streets throughout the city, think about the beloved ones close to your heart, and imagine how thankful you would be to the one who rescued them from the streets…

Before those brothers involved in crime, evaluate the hidden torture that would tear the bowels of your conscience, if you were in their place. Think about the gratitude you would devote to those who forgave your faults, supporting your steps from the shadows into the light.

Even when you find yourself alone, working for the good of the neighbor, and enduring the mockery of those temporarily lost in denial and selfishness, you will not be discouraged.

By believing in the mercy of the Divine Providence and the endless possibilities of human renewal, you will follow Jesus, the Master, and the Lord. He taught us all, with humility and abnegation, that the love and service in favor of our brothers and sisters are the only forces able to sublimate the intelligence, in order that the Kingdom of God definitely establishes in the domain of the heart.

3

Environments

Not only will we have what we give, but we will also live in what we give to others.

That is why it is necessary to do only the good, fully the good.

If at a certain range of time, we bring joy to the neighbor and cause them to suffer on another track, then we will divide our existence into happiness and misfortune. This happens because we have brought one and another to our conviviality, and then we ruin valuable opportunities of service and spiritual elevation.

If we give them bitterness, then clearly we will sour the feelings of those who welcome us, receiving in inevitable exchange the same negative vibrations; just like those who take the inconvenient water for their thirst, after stirring the bottom of the well, which they need.

If we throw criticism and irony on the face of the neighbor, then we will not have another situation to live, but that which heads for sarcasm and censorship.

We are sure that not only people, but also the environments respond to us. Whether we like it or not, we are constrained to live in the spiritual environment that we have created.

Let us pacify, and we will have peace.

Let us help, and we will receive help.

Spiritually speaking, everything that comes from us returns to us.

Jesus said: **"Give, and it will be given to you."**

Not only in the domain of the material donation, properly considered, does the teaching prevail. From what we give to others, life inevitably will give us.

4

A Step Up

The moral improvement and practice of goodness constitute the scenery of the walk forward into the Realm of the Spirit, but we must not forget that every obstacle is a marker of an opportunity for a step up, on the path of elevation.

In the educational establishment, test by test, the student completes his course to ensure his cultural learning.

In life's school, trial by trial, the soul acquires the necessary merit for the evolutionary climbing.

Every lesson brings an ennobling aim, which one should achieve through the study.

Therefore, any difficulty encloses a spiritual value that we ought to understand, in order to profit from it.

In any educational institution, many subjects are taught.

In every existence, the instructions reveal a different character.

This is how the time of the step-up occurs, with always new expressions, enabling us the assimilation of superior qualities in every sense.

The temptation is a step of access to the spiritual fortress.

A received insult is a chance to gain height by the trail of forgiveness.

A violent and painful act against us is an opportunity for the acquisition of humility.

Suffering is a path to obtain patience.

The need of the neighbor means the imperative to be useful to them.

When misunderstanding or intolerance emerges on others, then it has come to us the day of comprehension and serenity.

Do not be indignant or disheartened when tribulations arise. Despair and revolt, besides generating conflicts and tears, are among the most unfortunate responses we can give to the constructive challenges of life.

God would not send us problems if they were not necessary for us.

Every distress time is a time for the step up. It depends on us to continue accommodated in the shade, or to move courageously forward to obtain more light.

5

A Donation from the Heart

We all have something to offer, whether the money to relieve the needy, education to banish ignorance, help to remove difficulties or medicine to cure diseases.

There is, however, a gift that we all can share, without distinction, which costs nothing to those who give it and greatly benefits those who receive it: we are talking about the blessing of courage.

How many people fall from high rungs of goodness, being at the apex of resistance against the evil, because they lacked warmth through an affectionate and comprehensive phrase?

How many deserted their ennobling tasks with an evident loss to the community, on the very eve of a victorious achievement, only by missing someone to supplement their rickety moral strength with a friendly gesture?

How many fall daily into frustration or sickness, just because there is nothing but bitterness and pessimism in the words of the people they have to live together?

Not only with material resources should you arm yourself to fight misfortune, but also with a living faith and hope, comprehension and optimism, so your word becomes a saving light, able to rekindle the confidence of so many brothers of Humanity, whose heart is like a dead light in the chest.

Do not wait until tomorrow for the time to encourage the brothers and sisters on the path to practice the good.

Do it now. Open your soul to them and speak about their immortality, but speak also about the inexhaustible treasure of time, and the unlimited resources of the Universe.

Help them to recognize the infinite energy that they own, and also help them to unveil the divine inheritance of eternal life that palpitates in their innermost being, even when facing the worst experiences.

May your word be a gleam to sustain, a flame to heat, a balsam that restores, and support that protects.

Whenever you decide to leave your personal life for the labor of beneficence, do not forget the gift of courage!

Second your friend by all the right resources at your fingertips, but, above all, help the individual of any condition or any origin, to feel our real brother, so wanting of the patience and assistance of God as us.

6

Giving

The major transformations of life often proceed from the donations we make.

Giving, in essence, means opening paths, supporting opportunities, multiplying relationships.

Many still believe that the act of helping shall come exclusively from those who guarantee themselves on monetized powers.

Naturally, no one should underestimate the betterment that the donated or lent money can provide; nevertheless, it does not imply that the donation is a privilege of those transitorily called to the financial comfort in the world.

We all can distribute consolation, enthusiasm, kindness and encouragement.

Sometimes, just a smile is enough to sweep loneliness. A phrase of solidarity can set up a new life within the spirit in which pain has banished hope.

Strictly speaking, all the virtues have their roots in the act of giving. Beneficence is a donation of one's own resources. Patience is a donation of inner tranquility. Tolerance is a donation of understanding. Sacrifice is the donation of oneself.

Any donation put into circulation unfailingly returns to the donor, supplemented by always higher values.

Whoever wishes to bring more efficiency and development to his tasks and obligations, ought to strive to extend his resources to aid others, and he will notice without delay the fortunate results of such an undertaking.

This is because, in the entire Universe, the Divine Laws are based on love, which at the bottom is the omnipresence of God in eternal donations.

In any sum of prosperity and peace, realization and fulfillment, the service to benefit the neighbor is the most important part; moreover, it is the only one susceptible to sustain the other activities that make up the structure of success.

Give from what you have and can; give from what you are and represent, in the belief that your donation is an investment in life's organization, guaranteeing the withdrawal of resources and forces, which you may need along the way.

"Give, and it will be given to you" – the Christ of God taught us.

So only through the blessing of giving, may the life of each one of us become a godsend.

7

Your Place

There are shady moves in life, in which expendable afflictions visit our spirit, giving us the impression that we are out of our environment.

We wish thoughtlessly to do the function of another person, and, at the same time, ask others to command ours. This, however, would disrupt the Divine Order.

We are aware that the Emissaries of the Lord know us to spare the skills and resources. Just like the engineers responsible for buildings, the Organizers of Life would not assign to us positions that were strange to our possibilities in the construction of God's Kingdom.

Within this subject, we should not forget that the promotion is a natural occurrence that elevates our level, but only when we improve ourselves, conquering steps up, does the promotion appear.

Nevertheless, strictly speaking, it is imperative to realize that now we find ourselves precisely at the point and the post where we can produce more and better. Such certainty strengthens our concept of responsibility. This happens because, if we know that God has allowed us to fulfill the duties regarding others, we can focus attention and energy to give the best of ourselves in the social machine we are a part.

When discouraging thoughts come, saying that you should be in another angle, in the field of common activities, calm your heart, and remain faithful to the obligations that the circumstances prescribe for you. Recognize that each day we are in the place that the God's Goodness wants us to be for the general welfare.

Hence, if you bring good conscience in the accomplishment of your tasks, it is necessary to understand some important issues, so your hours are full of peace and efficiency in your sector of action, within the Work of the Lord:

You are today what you are, find yourself with whom you do, in the context where you move, and the way you express yourself, because God determines so. As it is just as you are, with whom and in the place you are, and just the way you find yourself, that the Lord needs you.

8

In Life's Account

Let compassion clean your eyes and lubricate your ears, so you can see and listen in the glory of good.

How many times we generate complications and exacerbate problems, only for demanding from others that of a hero and saint we still cannot do?

Let us try to react as we would like others to do, before misunderstandings or concerns if the difficulties were ours.

The Earth is full of those who censor and accuse.

Let us support us mutually.

Sometimes, in moments of irritation or hopelessness, you pronounce unfortunate words that you would like to recover, to make them useless, if possible, and you thank the goodness of the listener, that decides to throw them into the basket of oblivion. Therefore, why not acting such way when receiving a negative comment from someone in despair?

In unfair attitudes, thoughtless decisions or mistakes we make, we praise the mercy of those who give us kindness and understanding, extinguishing in silence the results of our unintentional faults.

How not to adopt the same standard of action when one of our brothers is sliding around in the shade?

We talk about the need for the soul's progress; we affirm the imperative of one's own improvement…

Let us start this meritorious effort in favor of ourselves by realizing that others carry trials and weaknesses just like ours, when they are not much more distressing problems and barriers.

Let us admire our fellows when they devote themselves to the good, or when they are in harmony with the good. On the other hand, whenever they slide into evil ways, let us treat them with the love we declare to cultivate with Jesus.

Any investment in the tolerance that we do to help the neighbor today, in the economic system of life, will be a precious deposit tomorrow, which we can use to help those we love most, or even in our own favor.

9

Before the Law of Good

Without a doubt, when afflictions succeed one another in life, we feel like a traveller lost in the jungle, by events summoned to build his own way.

When such an obscure moment arrives, in which crises emerge, generating crises, do not ascribe to someone else the blame for the embarrassing situation, nor allow pessimism to defeat you.

Reflect on the value of time, and do not use the potential power of minutes in the domain of the complaint and dissatisfaction. Pray, stand up to obstacles in thought, and work in favor of your own liberation, being sure that, behind the difficulties, the law of goodness is working.

Above all, be sure that God, Our Father, is the author and supporter of the Highest Good. No evil could change God's Supreme Government, which is based on infinite love and everlasting goodness. As a result, what seems to be a disease is, indeed, a health recovering process.

Small annoyances categorized by offences are invitations to review the hurdles placed on your path, or requests to pray for those brothers in Humanity, who rashly become persecutors of the good works that they are still unable to comprehend.

Setbacks seen as ingratitude of beloved ones, often only mean changes in the Superior Plans for the benefit of those we love, who are still creditors of our understanding and care.

Discord is a problem that asks for peace action. Household arguments are nothing but a demand for more dedication towards family members, so, we can definitely reconcile to opponents from the past, and suppress any possibility of a return to causes of suffering and imbalance that already brought us falls and obsessions in previous incarnations.

Also, the presence of death is nothing but more renewal and more life.

Whenever tribulations emerge, like sickness or grief, humiliation or penury, persecution or temptation, loss or disaster, do not surrender to revolt or dismay. Work and wait, between the pleasure of serving and the joy of trusting; bearing in mind that if you are looking for the relief of God, the help of God is also seeking for you.

And if tranquility seems to be late, because deprivation and trials multiply, then persevere with the service and hope, reminding that the law of goodness is always working, and the comfort of God is hidden or is about to come.

10

Personal Environment

Anywhere you step on, your individual aura flows.

Your words emanate the magnetism that springs from your heart.

We intend to help others according to the beneficence; however, one ought to know how doing it, once we offer ourselves instinctively in what we grant.

The gift always brings the influences of the donor.

Hence, analyze the reactions and thoughts you inspire, wherever, whenever and to whom you express yourself.

Any study in this sense can be done without any embarrassment, as long as you decide to see for yourself the results of the others' presence.

At the time of insecurity, do not appreciate the conversation of those who do not understand you. On the days of illness, do not accept the depressing views of those who poison themselves with pessimism.

The voice that impels you to build the virtue is a blessing of infinite value, but the one that censors the defect in extinction is a mental jolt of unforeseeable consequences.

Do not make silence where events await your presence, but study the situation before presenting yourself, so that no unfortunate attitude on your part spoils the fruitful results that your intervention should produce.

Understanding first, acting afterward.

The need demands help, but if it comes disorderly, then the need becomes greater.

Meditate upon the spiritual atmosphere that you bring, and cultivate serenity, in order that serenity composes your environment.

This is neither about doing calculated charity, nor practicing the good under principles of mathematics, but practicing respect for life everywhere, by cultivating love.

11

Your Mind

Among the treatments due to the body and soul, let us remember the problem of housing.

The more a person is educated, the cleaner is their residence. Sometimes a house is not rich from the material point of view. One can see there, however, cleanliness and order, security and good taste.

Not only in the external home should the sense of hygiene and harmony be used, but also in the inner life of each one.

The mind is the home of the soul.

As it happens to any house, it has many rooms for several activities, but sometimes, we burden the rooms of our inner home with ideas that result very inadequate to the real necessities.

When encysted prejudices, useless theories, afflictions and fears, complaints and hurts install inside, we embezzle the treasures of time and opportunities for growth, as we hinder the way of the transforming flow of life through our own forces.

We know that the house, no matter how humble it is, must be sunny and aired to ensure a good health of its inhabitants.

No one keeps garbage in the household environment on purpose.

If there are problems in the electrical energy or sewage system, it demands urgent repair.

Since remote times, we have fought the darkness. From the torch to the hanging oil lamp, and from the oil lamp to the modern bulb, human beings have struggled to create resources to defend against the predominance of darkness.

Consider this and do not keep resentments, nor cultivate contentions in the field of your soul.

Work, study, do the good and forget the evil, in order to regiment against the mist of ignorance.

Your Mind: your inalienable home. Here dreams and aspirations, emotions and thoughts, plans and accomplishments are born. From your mind come your manifestations on the life paths and on our demonstrations on the paths of life depend the captivity to the shadow or the liberation towards the light.

12

Towards the Kingdom of God

Certainly, Jesus has been with us since the beginning, in the building of God's Kingdom, and thus, we urgently need to realize that he does not ask from us demonstrations of heroism or spectacles of greatness for this purpose.

Everything in such edification is understandable and simple, but for such reason, the Master hopes that we meet our simple and understandable tasks, in the regimen of the most effort, so we can collaborate in the foundation of the eternal structure.

In order to reach the Kingdom of God in this world, the Lord does not demand from us pilgrimages of sacrifice to particular regions. Despite this, Jesus expects us to show enough courage to live day by day, in the accurate fulfillment of the duties while on the difficult journey of incarnation.

He does not want from us a degree in the grammatical rules of the language in which we enjoy the privilege of understanding. However, he wishes that we say the wise and comforting words in favor of the brothers and sisters of Humanity, whenever necessary.

He does not compel us to renounce to material goods. Nevertheless, he hopes that we administrate them sensibly, employing the possible remaining in relief to the brethren in shortage.

He does not impel us to engage in a unique training for the premature development of physical or psychical forces, but he wants us to strain to hinder negative thoughts and dominate bad inclinations.

He does not ask us to reach the moral perfection from one day to the next; in spite of this, he expects that we cooperate with him, tolerating invectives and forgetting them, in favor of the general welfare.

He does not ask from us sacrificial feeding systems or a way of life incompatible with fair and natural needs, but he hopes that we respect the physical body we received from the Law of Reincarnation, keeping constantly faithful to the commitments that we assumed one before the others.

He does not recommend us the social withdrawal under the excuse of preserving qualities to the heavenly glory; though, he wants us to bring kindness, forgiveness, patience and love into our social life, so that, little by little, we comprehend that we are all brothers before the same Father.

Jesus does not ask us for the impossible; he calls for collaboration and work, only to the extent of our human possibilities. It is a responsibility, however, to consider that if we all look forward to the Happy World of Tomorrow, we must remember that as a building rises from the base, the Kingdom of God begins with us.

13

From Sunrise to Sunset

You claim to be facing a difficult time, in which bad events come in droves, compelling you to the most severe tests of moral strength.

So complex is the mass of conflicts in the spiritual sphere that many of the brothers and sisters on the evolutionary journey rather stay in the rearward, searching for redoing, or the cure of sick nerves.

Therefore, you often ask yourself how to work efficiently while resisting with success the siege of restlessness. It involves a very important issue in the spiritual life of each one, once neither can we be inactive in the field of action, nor can we ignore the need for balance, in order to endure with patience the trials that arise on the path.

The only solution is to focus the mind and heart on the Spirit of the Lord, and he, the Divine Master, will make the work productive, and bring the rest to our hearts.

Before an unforeseen difficulty, trust him with the obstacles, and keep doing the duty embraced.

When confronted with an unexpected tribulation, imagine his vigorous hands in yours and try to overcome it with determination, enjoying the blessed lessons of suffering.

Whenever challenging problems emerge, trust God with your problems, and patiently meet the responsibilities that life has reserved for you.

If friends have deserted you, think of him as the unfailing friend, and keep loyal to the commitments that dignify your life.

Let us share every day the blessed burden of work that weighs on our shoulders with the Christ of God. He is the manager of every elevation company, and the provider partner of all our needs.

Let the Lord do the work you cannot do and go forward, providing the best resources at your reach in the performance of the immediate tasks that you have undertaken.

By doing so, you will notice that any troubles will dissipate around you, as the shadows crumble in the light of heaven, so you work cheerfully on the well-being of everyone, with invariable serenity, from sunrise to sunset.

14

Trials of Beloved Ones

In the daily routine, not only do we have our difficulties, but also those related to our dear ones, for whom we often suffer much more than for ourselves.

However, it is crucial to know that as we intend to support those cherished hearts, we are never alone, for God, Who has lent them to our conviviality, remains watching, without forgetting them.

On days of grey and shade of trials, let us devote ourselves to our objects of love with all our gentleness, but avoiding filling them with anxiety or restlessness, sadness or mistrust.

If they ask us for advice, let us not wander to personal suggestions, but help them to seek for the Divine Inspiration through prayer, as God knows their needs and will draw a safe route for their behavior.

If they are sick, it is more than fair to provide them attention and consideration; though, let us commit ourselves to lead their thoughts towards optimism; being sure that God protects their existence in every heartbeat.

If they make changes in their lives, we should refrain from interfering in their decisions whatsoever, but instead, let us strive to bless them in their plans for renewal and development, being sure that the Divine Providence watches over us and guides their steps.

If they slip on harsh trials, we should work to relieve and release them, for it is a duty, but without torturing them with our unconformity and distress, being sure that God is not absent from the part of the regenerative or edifying struggles that we all must withstand in some ranges of time.

Let us help the objects of our tenderness to be authentic, as they are and as they should be towards life.

Arguably, as problems arise in our path, many other problems appear in the field of action of the endeared ones. Even so, in order to aid them with efficiency and security, we should work in their favor based on love and balance, recognizing that we are not alone in this rescuing job, once long before us, God has worked on the case of each one.

15

You will follow the Light

You will recognize the divine potential of the human heart, not only to cultivate gratitude but also in order not to disappoint the expectations of the Master and Lord, who allowed you to bring his name on the facade of the commitments.

Many will say that humanity has reached the moral bankruptcy, and that civilizations have gone backwards; that the evil invaded the dwellings, and there is no good to do anymore…

Nevertheless, you will continue believing in the human being and his infinite capacity for renewal and sublimation.

Many will fall away. You will serve, loyal to your post, wherever you are.

You will forget the prophets of desolation and the preachers of misery, who spend the treasure of hours buying regret with the corrupted words about the problems of the Earth in transition.

You will accomplish the duties you have taken upon yourself, even before the imperative of suffocating your reactions in the face of evil, once it would only favor the chaos.

You will arm yourself with understanding and self-denial, tolerance and conformity, so you may be among the soldiers of God, who support the constant and centuries-old battle of the human being against the forces of darkness.

You will inspire yourself in those, whom the peoples of today own their stability and greatness, and you will remember these millions of unknown apostles!

Of the teachers who put out their light, so their students glowed.

Of the parents who forgot themselves among the home walls, so their offspring could grow up, contributing to the creation of a better world.

Of the ones who kept gold without selfishness, employing it judiciously in cooperation to the work and development, beneficence and education.

Of those who offered themselves as a sacrifice to science, so that the hospitals could uphold life against death.

Of those who gave up personal comfort to dedicate themselves to the word or the feather, in tiresome schedules and without compensation in this life, so enlightenment and solace were not scarce to the general mind.

Of the ones who left the body, faithful to the duties that they embraced in favor of others, though they could have rested on the days approaching death, by the imposition of physical exhaustion.

Of those who voluntarily took upon their shoulders the duties of others who defected from good deeds.

The ones who did not allow that offence and misunderstandings, slanders or unfair accusations stopped the work of helping the neighbor!

Not only will you remember these righteous that have kindled the light upon your path, but you will also follow them, loving and serving always!

You will banish the evil with goodness, and violence with patience; you will extinguish hatred with love, and undo the censorship with the blessing.

Although your feet bleed, hike with them, the anonymous heroes of the Eternal Goodness, the steep path of the ascension, being certain that in front of all these pioneers of the winning immortality, goes Jesus, the Exalted Friend, who one day promised us clearly and safely:

"He who follows Me shall not walk in darkness."

16

The Effect of Forgiveness

Among the aspects of forgiveness, there is one we should emphasize, due to its importance: its results within ourselves, when we have the fortune of forgiving.

We generally understand forgiveness as a simple act of virtue and generosity in favor of the offender, who would rely on the absolute magnanimity of the victim. However, it often happens that the victim does not always know how far the offender will benefit from this liberality, once we cannot penetrate the innermost being of one another. In addition, on the other hand, the good determines to relegate to oblivion the debris of all wickedness.

Nevertheless, we must understand that when we forgive someone's mistake or provocation against us, we disclaim evil of any compromise with us while we untangle ourselves of all the links susceptible to attach us to it.

Consider such reality and do not carry along the explosive of hatred or the poison of grief, which destroys life and corrode the organic forces, throwing the individual into the ditch of sickness or unjustified death.

You will frequently experience the intrusion of darkness into your way, especially if you devote yourself with diligence and decision to the harvest of good; but do not welcome and take it with you, just like a blade buried in your heart with your own hands.

Before any offences, pacify, defend, and restore yourself, forgiving always.

On the tracks of life, when we entrench ourselves in the hardness of the soul, we are those who first and more intensively suffer the results of intolerance.

Without a doubt, when we practice forgiveness, it is impossible to know if one properly accepted it, or if it produced the benefits we wished it to do. Despite this, whenever we forgive the affront done to us, we can readily see the beneficial effects of forgiveness in our hearts, in the form of balance and peace acting in us.

17

Hidden Heroism

You may have heard about sublime deeds, in which intrepid people offered their own lives to save others. We can mention, for instance, those who perished defending communities, in honor of Justice, and those who were surprised by an unexpected death, in praise of Science, investigating minutely relief processes of human suffering.

Yes, we should revere the name of those who forgot themselves in favor of the neighbor. However, there is an obscure heroism, as authentic and beautiful as that which marks the protagonists of great exploits in face of death. We talk about the hidden heroism of those who know how to live, day by day, within the narrow circle of obligations, in spite of the obstacles and trials that torture them.

Think of it, when the embarrassments of life embitter your heart…

You can be sure that if there are crowds on Earth to applaud the demonstrations of courage, from those who die for noble causes, there are crowds in the spiritual world to applaud the testimonies of comprehension and sacrifice of people who live to help the neighbor, darkening themselves little by little, aiming at someone's uplift, or the development of some people in the earthly arena.

Reflect on it and think about the most difficult part of the existence that God has entrusted to you...

Is it perhaps the captivity to undelayable household obligations, the inner conflict, or the laborious guardianship of a sick child, a brother or sister; alternatively the permanent tolerance towards the husband or wife in imbalance, or the direct and personal responsibility for works of merit and culture, elevation, and harmony in the job of managing communities?

School enrollment in silent heroism is constantly open to us all.

We remember the words of the Divine Master: *"If anyone would come after me, let him deny himself and take up his cross and follow me."*

What and how will be the cross that weighs on your shoulders?

Whatever it is, remember that the Christ of God awaits us on the mountain of victory and redemption, hoping that we will have enough courage to embrace the hidden heroism, faithful to our own duties, until the end.

18

Between God and the Neighbor

For all of us who teach to learn and learn to teach evangelical conduct lessons in prayer groups, there is a problem that we must courageously face: the problem of practicing the redemptive or regenerating theories that we have embraced.

Within the circle of prayer, we receive the orientation, and beyond it, we ought to bring it to our behavior. High thoughts, and actions that correspond to them. Good words and good works. We should remain at home under the same guidelines that we adopt in the temple of faith.

We often assume that it is very difficult, and we believe we can take two different attitudes: one with which we properly attend church, through prayer, and the other one in which we frequently use of carelessness when we relate to the brothers and sisters.

Even so, it is necessary to understand that God is everywhere, and everywhere we must behave as someone who is in the Divine Presence.

The Creator meets the creature both in prayer and in action.

In prayer, we are induced to understanding and mildness, because we reliably ask for the Mercy of Heavens, waiting for tolerance and love for our needs. Nevertheless, it is essential to remember that the Mercy of Heavens listens and supports us with infinite goodness, in order that we use this same process of aid and blessing for other people's needs.

What is the point in showing a sweet face to God and a bitter heart to the fellows in the daily struggle, if all of them are also sons of God as we?

If we still cannot transfer the environment of prayer to our work sphere, then let us strain to conquer the sublime and indispensable achievement.

The supplication before the Lord compares to a check based on the capital of service to our brothers in Christ.

Thus, let us learn to start living before God, in the light of the duties towards the neighbor, and living before the neighbor recalling the obligations towards God.

19

Firmness and Gentleness

On the daily journey, there is an urgent need to harmonize the expressions of our qualities with the spirit of proportion and profit, so the extremism does not impose on us accidents in the development of relationships and activities.

We must have energy in faith, but not too much that it becomes fanaticism.

Gentleness in goodness; nevertheless, not too much that it shows carelessness.

Energy in conviction; yet not too much that it becomes stubbornness.

Mildness in humility; even so, not too much that it degenerates in servility.

Energy in the justice; however, not too much that it turns into cruelty.

Mildness in kindness; but not too much that it reveals flattery.

Energy in sincerity; nevertheless, not too much that it slides towards disrespect.

Mildness in peace; yet not too much that it accommodates in laziness.

Strength in courage; though, not too much that it becomes temerity.

Mildness in prudence; but not too much that it turns into self-indulgent.

On the path of life, one should learn from the very life.

Let us take a look at the modern automobile in today's travels; neither is it slow, for that would mean ignoring the progress of the engine, nor beyond the fair speed limits, which would cause accidents and premature deaths.

We should have the balance in everything since if we have the balance, in everywhere and every time we will guarantee in ourselves the charity and patience; the two guardians able to ensure us a safe route and a happy arrival.

20

Above us

How many times we seek for peace, experiencing the torture of the thirsty that yearns for glory...

In such moments, the most significant step will be always our unconditional surrender to God, whose wisdom will lead us in the direction of the industrious and invigorating tranquility.

It is imperative to think about it, once unexpected crises often arise in the daily life, enveloping our minds in the form of problems considered insoluble within the framework of the human providences.

On many occasions, you did everything you could to sustain a beloved one on the firm ground of higher ideals, and though, you had to see his abrupt fall into the precipices of shadow...

You have given the best values of life for the happiness of someone, who accepted it while it gave them immediate benefits, and one moment to another you have suffered an unspeakable neglect, receiving offence and sarcasm in exchange for renunciation and love...

You have taken the responsibility of a friend who left you alone in a maze of disturbing business and commitments, without any consideration for your testimonials of confidence...

You have given the best of you to protect the familiar group for a long time of work and sacrifice, and, suddenly, you were under the scorn of the same relatives that owed you affection and respect, without the slightest possibility of a claim...

Before any difficulties and above all, in times of a supreme bitterness, entrust the Divine Providence with the hardships that flog your soul!

In the condition of human beings, all of us, evolving Spirits on the Planet, do not always have enough energy to overcome our deficiencies...

Therefore, in terrible and distressed times of adversities, do not surrender to despair! Search the infinite credits of the Infinite Love Father.

None of us is an orphan of support and relief, light, and blessing, as even when all the forces fail, in the service of good, in the performance of our obligations, greatly above us and far above our limited and fragile resources, we have God.

21

Disturbances and Obsession

In the daily experience, there always comes a moment when we ask ourselves at what point we are about the spiritual misfit, and if we are not in total disharmony, we often find ourselves in clear perturbation.

This is because, according to the principle that nobody is totally impassive, we have an emotional life permanently threatened by external challenges, as unpleasant episodes or upsetting news that represents to us a measure of balance and resistance in the moral struggle we have to endure, in favor of our own enlightenment.

If before this or that unfortunate event, we usually forget systematically patience and resignation, understanding and serenity, then it is necessary to take a time for reflection, on the mind mechanisms, so we can develop the required rectifications in ourselves.

In such circumstances, we often think about obsession, assuming we are victims of vampire spirits.

The problem, however, is not limited to the opponents' influence, which is inserted in our psychic waves, but it mainly refers to us.

We fell into deep abysses of hatred and vengeance, despair and crime in many situations of previous incarnations, operating in wide periods of time against ourselves, and compromising our destinies.

Thus, we find the imperative of regenerative and bitter, though, essential experiences, just like it happens to a delayed student, who needs further examination in the tests of grade repetition.

In view of such considerations, whenever our feelings turn uncontrolled, let us safely take the ship's helm of our thoughts, in the tide of life trials, in the peace of meditation and the silence of prayer.

Through the self-control, we will watch the door of the manifestations, blocking out inadvisable gestures and words, and with the help of prayer, we will do light to understand what happens to us, so we can prevent a fall into alienation and turmoil.

Let us dedicate constantly to this work of mental self-immunization, once, next to an immense number of disturbed and obsessed brothers and sisters who swarm the Earth today, we see everywhere thousands of people almost at the gates of obsession.

22

You will be Patient

You will be patient. You will understand that we do not always obtain the provision of assistance through material resources; though, you will see that the patience, the daughter of charity, has a free passport to work with the needed success in overcoming any obstacles to the achievement of good works.

Effectively, hatred and persecution, slander and evil, annihilate daily many edifying works on Earth, but it is imperative to remember that if they do not destroy even more, it is due to the faithful workers' patience, which opposes them a barrier through prayer and tolerance, defending from their attacks.

Patience!

Very often we believe it benefits exclusively us, when we have the good luck to follow its savior advices; however, it is a power of the soul, radiating whenever we practice this blessing, generating security and peace in favor of others, anywhere it expresses itself.

In order to know its opportunity and greatness, it would be necessary to visit the depths of suffering, where are gathered all those who were unable or unwilling to accommodate its presence in the heart.

Only there, in these workshops of rectification on the Earth and outside of it, could we see the number of people who threw themselves into crime and suicide, madness and death, for lack of a few minutes of patience; the infallible benefactor, in whose environment of comprehension, God assures us the gift of understand and wait.

You will remember this, and you will assist with the serenity of your life, there, where the fire of disharmony or rebelliousness is.

You will distribute the shares of your patience in any place you are, ensuring peace and optimism, light and good cheer to the sustaining of the love that the Divine Master instituted as the foundation for the Kingdom of God.

You will give from your patience to the sufferers and disoriented in the world; as much as you give from your pitcher to the thirsty, and distribute the benefits of your bread to the hungry.

You will indefinitely exercise the patience of listening, renewing, forgiving, learning, assisting, repeating...

You can be sure that by doing so, not only will you help yourself and those around you, but also the Lord, who does not need our honors, but he expects from each one of us, the support of patience, so he can use us in any problem, as an important part of the solution.

23

Ideals and Action

In fact, we must consider the value of reincarnation to assimilate its benefits.

Once aware that the physical body compares to the rehabilitation cell, the apron, or the study desk, it is necessary to know the importance of time, employing diligence in the accomplishment of obligations as a standard action, in the daily routine.

What would happen to a sick person, if someone dear took the unpleasant, but necessary medicines in his place, under the pretext of saving him an inconvenience?

What would be of a student, who relegated the responsibilities of taking his exams to more learned friends, under the excuse of finding kindness and favor?

Therefore, in the sphere of all experiences - especially in the field of the social ones - we learn to expect from the Lord the necessary power to fulfill the duties that circumstances have brought us, along with the gifts of health and labor, guidance and joy.

Sublime is charity, but if we have no inclination to practice it, this precious virtue will be nothing, but an ideal of Heaven, unable to land on Earth.

Divine is humility. Nevertheless, if we fail to suffer patiently, it will be only a shining and useless idea, as it does not emanate from the soul.

So is faith, goodness, tolerance…

Without the firmness of purpose to express them, they are solely dreams that fade away, with no connection with reality.

We mention that to say that both in problems of material and Spiritual Life, we need to ask God for the required instruments to conquer understanding and security, growth and harmony, which His Infinite Love directs to us by the blessings of life. Even so, it is necessary to ask for something else…

We must pray to Him, the Merciful God, to grant us the courage to live, and know how to live.

24

Forgiveness in the Familiar Environment

When we talk about forgiveness, we usually remember the classical picture, in which we are beside supposed opponents, distributing magnanimity and goodwill, as if we could live without other people's tolerance.

However, this issue spreads in various angles, notably those that refer to everyday life.

If we cannot forgive the faults of those we love, and if we are not excused for the mistakes we make against them, the common existence will be frankly impractical, for bitterness and irritations properly added up would achieve enough shares to bring premature death to anyone.

We need more forgiveness at home than in the social area, and more reciprocal cooperation in the atmosphere we serve the Lord than in the world's noisy avenues.

For our own benefit, we all need to cultivate understanding and constructive support within the systematic assistance to neighbors and family members, bosses and subordinates, customers and partners. We also need to have constant respect to the private life of close friends and tolerance towards dear ones; with patience and forgetfulness before any offences that hurt the hearts.

We should not expect calamitous occurrences, pain, and humiliation in public squares in order to appear in the position of dramatized benevolence actors, though the obligation to do the good and forget the evil, anywhere.

Let us learn to forgive, but sincerely, in heart and memory, all pinpricks and setbacks, annoyances and upsets, in the narrow circle of our personal relationships, exercising real goodness, in order to be really good.

Only then will we succeed in practicing the forgiveness that Jesus taught us. If the Master recommended that we forgive the enemies seventy times seven, then how many times should we forgive the friends who interweave our joy of living?

Certainly, the Master was silent on the reason why our fellows need us as much as we need them. Thus, with our hearts entwined on the path of life, it is imperative to understand that among true friends, any event will be a reason to learn safely to bless and understand, to help and love.

25

Divine Seeds

When someone tells you about the big amount of resources needed to settle human needs, do not underestimate the little you are able to do to help your neighbor, sharing the heart into pieces of understanding and love.

The dish of fraternal relief does not solve the problem of hunger, but it may be today the blessing that will reinvigorate the energies of someone on the verge of starvation, in order that the work tomorrow may move his steps away from the fog of disenchantment and distress.

The clothes for the neighbor in tatters does not solve the problem of nakedness, but it can be today the real help in favor of someone flogged by the cold weather, and who tomorrow will become a living fountain of sustenance for the homeless of the Earth.

The ennobling book placed in the hands of a friend in difficulty does not solve the problem of ignorance; though, it can be today the providential light to someone enveloped by the shadows, who tomorrow will be a radiant core of renewing ideas for thousands of people thirsty for direction and peace.

The quick minutes of an enlightening conversation, with a fellow entangled on the screens of bad influences do not solve the problem of obsession; nevertheless, this can be today the saving anchor to somebody threatened by a disturbance, who will become tomorrow a living example of spiritual education, redeeming the sufferers in the world.

Do not underestimate the crumb of cooperation with which one can encourage the sustaining of the good works. Remember the widow's mite, highlighted by Jesus as the richest donation to the services of faith, due to the sacrifice it represented. Not only that; let us remember the day the Lord blessed the five loaves and two fishes and fed an extensive crowd of hungry people.

In fact, any crumbs with us or simply by us will always be crumbs, but if we take it to the practice of goodness with Jesus, they will be divine seeds of peace and joy, education and progress, beneficence and prosperity in the whole world.

26

Attacks on Good Works

In the field of good works, a problem emerges from time to time, demanding from us patience and reflection:

The problem of attacks.

We agree that the brothers and sisters more particularly called to serve in the harvest of the Master are the most intensively watched by incessant and general observation.

So, we often look after them rigorously, as we hope to see them without any unfortunate moment.

It is easy to see that usually, each of us among those who lead and obey, yearns to find people as perfect as possible. If we are in a subaltern position, we want to have a boss just like a crystalline mirror of good examples, and if we are in commanding positions, here we are competing for cooperators, sometimes more efficient than ourselves.

However, there comes a day when the imperfections and weaknesses emerge on them, once they are inherent to us all, spirits in evolution in Humanity, and the ideal clashes with reality.

When unprepared, we throw ourselves to censorship without noticing it, and in many circumstances, we threaten the stability of the tasks we love most, just like a crazy sculptor who demanded a masterpiece from one moment to the next, striking the marble thoughtlessly.

When the attacks to noble accomplishments occur, we can see that they aim at those fellows who work and bring the best of all. As a matter of fact, in reputable realizations, there is no time to waste with brothers voluntarily extended in inertia.

Therefore, in moments of criticism, let us dedicate a minute of prayer, for the Lord will illuminate us, inspiring our attitude. If there is an error to correct, we will achieve the touch of charity to remedy it in the rectification.

If we feel mistreated, we will immediately forgive any offences, multiplying the forces in the necessary abnegation.

If we're attacking someone, we will learn soon, to identify the "good side" of the person, situation, event or circumstance that we worry about, in the uplifting cause to which we have committed to the heart.

When the attack comes, whatever it is, let us turn to the sustenance of goodness and the appeal of prayer, for prayer and mercy will bring us a ray of light from the Divine Mind, teaching us to see and understand, support and harmonize, help and serve.

27

Difficult Companions

Difficult companions are not the people with whom we still have no intimacy, but those who have won our love and suddenly changed thoughts and behavior, causing us surprise and preoccupation.

They used to be pillars of faith and submerged in heavy streams of temptations…

They shined like beacons of light ahead of the march, and they lost their light in the night of personal conveniences, propelling us to the shade and confusion…

Despite this, as we analyze the issue with discernment and serenity, would it be fair to shelter pessimism or disenchantment, solely because this or that friend has shown human weaknesses, which is also peculiar to us?

Considering the realities of the evolving sphere, where we carry burdens of guilt and debts, imperfections and needs, which have stuck on our shoulders in past lives, how could we demand from our dear ones, who breathe the same level as us, the state of the heroes or the behavior of angels?

By saying that, we do not mean that the omission or desertion of those to whom we have devoted trust and love are natural conditions for the spiritual work we must develop. As we regret their unhappy decisions, it is imperative to pray for them, on the guidelines of fraternal tolerance, with which we should embrace all of those who share with us the tasks of life journey.

If Jesus urged us to love the enemies, which rule should we adopt before difficult companions, other than blessing them at a higher level of understanding, as needy of a more extensive dedication as they show themselves?

Without a doubt, on many occasions, they may not share so quick our daily activities, due to the different commitments they have taken. Nevertheless, in the spirit's atmosphere, we will thank them for the good they have done to us, and what they can do, by addressing them the silent message of our respect and affection, encouragement and gratitude.

By doing such duty, we will find enough inner peace to go forward, in the fulfillment of the tasks with which life has entrusted us.

We understand that if the Lord accepts us as we are, tolerating our faults and leveraging us in service according to our capacity of being useful, then it is our obligation to accept our difficult fellows as they are, waiting for them, in terms of elevation or rectification, as much as the Lord has waited for us.

28

Judgments

As we watch the actions of others, it is important to remember that they also notice ours. Even so, we know from experience, that in many events of life, there is a huge distance between our intentions and our demonstrations.

How many times are we regarded as insensible and ungrateful, because we took a firm course of action in the social sphere, after long-time difficulties, when we harmed even other people's interests?

How many times did people take us for a coward because we were optimist or benevolent to whom we reached the limit of tolerance?

How many occasions have we been evaluated as cruel disciplinarians, when we only wish the defense and the victory of those we love most?

How many other times people have called us irresponsible and frivolous parents, when we allowed dear ones to face the difficult trials they chose, so invoking the freedom the Universe Laws give to each one?

Reflect on it and do not judge your neighbor by appearances. Let love inspire you at any comment, and when you have to say any remark, as part of a rectification process, put yourself in the place of the fellow under censorship. Thereafter, you will find the right words to cooperate in the work of unlimited mercy, with which God operates all the constructions and modifications.

Correct by loving, what must be corrected and restore by serving what should be restored. However, never condemn, once the Lord will find means of invalidating the evil positions, so that goodness prevails, and whenever circumstances require you to check other people's acts, remember that our actions are also being checked.

29

Emotional Disturbances

As we linger incarnated on Earth, we experience a subtle kind of impatience, which can drag us to the worst emotional disturbances: the revolt against ourselves.

We accept unfounded fears, based on opinions that people formulate about us, whether because of physical deformities, organic frustrations, psychological conflicts or social issues we may present, and we adopt the fear as a standard action, in exaggerated esteem for ourselves, and from this systematic concern, commonly emerges a continuous displeasure against the living forces intertwined in our physical vehicle.

We attack mentally these resources so much, that we end up neurotic, fatigued, sick or obsessed, mechanically slipping to the gutter of premature death.

This is all due to a lack of patience with our trials or imperfections.

Surely, nobody is born in the physical body to praise the deficiencies they take along, or to enlarge them, but we need to accept ourselves as we are, and give the best of us.

A constructive self-confidence. Understanding of the lesson that lies ahead. We ought to welcome the physical instrument that the High Command of Life considers necessary for us, both for redemption from faults of our past and the achievements for the general well-being, doing all the good we can.

Your carnal body or your social-familiar landscape is the best tool and right place, indispensable to the regenerative trial or the specific mission you should dedicate yourself. Thus, the sore point of existence is the hard test that exercises your moral resistance, so shaping your person on your way toward a greater service in the future.

Our emotional disturbances almost always arise from our reluctance to accept some of the less agreeable aspects of our life, despite their temporary condition.

Hence, let us live with them courageously, honestly.

Nothing of subterfuges. Do we have a body with deficiencies, or are we in a position vulnerable to criticism? Let it be.

In contrast to this, however, let us consider that nobody is an orphan of the Father's Goodness, and putting ourselves in the Hands of the Almighty, let us try to achieve all of good or beautiful in our circle of work.

On the other hand, it is worth saying that admitting the existence of an error or maladjustment in us is a sign of development and progress. The spirits embedded in inertia do not see their own moral needs. They accommodate themselves to the supposed satisfaction of the senses, which anaesthetize their conscience until the pain awakens them, so they resume the effort they should do on the journey of evolution and improvement.

Therefore, let us thank for the spiritual light we already have to analyze our personality, and embracing the tasks of balance or rehabilitation we should do inside ourselves, let us face our obstacles with serenity and patience, being sure that we can solve all the problems in the workshop of service, with the blessing of God.

## 30

Fortune

Money left over can easily guarantee the relief work and the presence of joy. It is impossible to predict the extent of happiness that may come from the currency that the fraternal assistance transubstantiates into blessings of light.

However, though we know that money is an agent of support and consolation, do not be willing to conquer it mercilessly.

On many occasions, you want to trust yourself to the service of good, and so you ask the Lord to fill you with gold and silver reserves; nevertheless, just like it happens to any set of coordinated knowledge for higher goals in life, altruism and beneficence need preparation and beginning.

The inks, which in the artist's hands configure the panel, a creator of renewing emotions in the soul, can make the stain that disfigures the wall, when in the fingers that ignore the intimacy with the beautiful.

Those who possess money without enrolling in the discipline of renunciation and goodness cannot achieve anything, but the martyrdom of the covetous, who dry the sources of life in their own being.

They keep substantial economic ballast, but they are slaves of avariciousness, in which many times, while enjoying the reincarnation, they transform their descendants in orphans of living parents, to transfigure them after death, in models of wastefulness and madness, by the mechanisms of inheritance.

Strive to deserve your extra money properly, so you spread generosity and progress along your days, but build on the ground of the spirit the understanding and solidarity, in order to use it with security and discernment.

Fortune, as much as it occurs with power and authority, demands balance and orientation to favor efficiently. Moreover, if you want to be helpful in the ideal of blessing and elevating, helping and serving, it is essential not to forget that all of us, in all climates and corners of the Earth, have received from God the endless riches of love, in the living treasure of heart.

# 31

Other Enemies

Oftentimes we hear that the exterior enemies are the worst exponents of disturbance that work to our detriment.

In spite of this, it is imperative to look inside ourselves to discover that the most difficult opponents are those that we cannot move easily, as they are in our innermost being.

Among them, the most ruthless are:

Selfishness, which hobbles our spiritual vision, preventing us from seeing the needs of those we love most;

The pride, which blocks the light of understanding and throws us to a permanent unbalance;

The vanity, which suggests the overestimation of our value, leading us to despise the worthiness of others;

The discouragement, which impels us to the chasms of inertia;

The mental intemperance, which places us in the domains of indiscipline;

The fear of suffering, which takes away from us the best progress opportunities; and many other harmful agents that install in our spirit, corroding energies and depredating the mental stability.

For the transformation of opponents, we usually count on the support of friends, who help us to review relationships, assisting us in the creation of new paths; however, to eliminate those that live inside ourselves, it is only the aid of God, with our own laborious effort.

When reporting to outer enemies, Jesus warned us that we must forgive offenses seventy times seven, and assuredly to get rid of internal enemies - all of them born in the darkness of ignorance - the Lord promised us:

"You will know the truth, and the truth will set you free."

This means that we will only be safe from our inner disasters through hard work, in the workshop of education.

32

Speaking and Listening

Let us never forget the creative power of speech.

The words you say are spoken with the full force of what you are; so, the problem is not only a matter of talking, but talking aiming at the good, with the pruning of every inconvenient for the balance or safety of the neighbor.

Precious is the ministry of those who suppress the material penury, and sublime will always be the apostolate of those who teach, dissolving the mist of ignorance; despite this, equally worthy is the work of those who facilitate the path of others.

Any of us can remove a danger on the streets, or uproot the poisonous plant on the home ground, attentive to the responsibility in the community life.

How could we not help a fellow of daily life, by keeping silent about a comment able to embitter his life, as thirsty for peace as ours?

It does not mean that we should have disagreements with those friends who still often talk unaware of the spiritual realities. Simply install the filter of comprehension within the acoustics of the soul.

It is fair to eliminate from our relationships with others, everything that traumatizes our feelings since the golden rule should be called to legislate on the subject so that we do not talk to others what we do not want others to tell us.

Above all, let us consider the equipment with which the Divine Wisdom has clothed us for the control of verbal resources: two eyes, two ears, but solely one mouth. Before a word is foreshadowed on the lips, we have the impulses of the heart projected to the brain, and inside the brain, these same impulses change into thoughts, likely to undergo a rigorous selection, just like it happens to the foods at home.

Let us check all the thoughts that come into the mind, and just like we reject rotten potatoes, every time that unedifying ideas arise, let us turn off the sockets of attention, in order to employ distance and oblivion with them.

33

Beloved Family

When talking about family, it is easy to realize that from the share of time you have spent with anxiety feelings in life, perhaps the largest part was taken up with concerns around them.

Parents, children, husbands and wives, brothers and sisters, and friends! Many of them might be in trouble... Threatened. Unhappy. They may have suffered temptations, endured losses; feeling disoriented, tormented by affliction and discouragement.

In view of the trials undergone, they probably show behavior changes, and maybe they have fallen into mistakes and mazes, whose obscure meanders they will spend a long time to overcome...

In these critical times of common experience, you often ask yourself: "What should I do to help them?"

First of all, be sure that it will not be by regretting or accusing that you will make yourself useful, neither by giving up your own responsibilities to follow their steps, in the inadvisable attempt to take them from the edifying struggles they need.

In an effort to help them, let us remind ourselves, when we were set in certain crossroads of the world, admitting that seldom did we follow the noble warnings with which people advised us.

Let us recall the occasions on which we archived worthy opinions, and silenced before seizures of dear souls, without absolutely neglecting inclinations and purposes, which were taking us to inconvenient actions and adventures.

Whenever you must endure a long absence of beloved people, for they have chosen paths that you cannot share, remember that they are looking for their own realization.

Instead of strangeness or censorship, give them the valuable support of your understanding and blessing.

In addition, you can help them through prayer, remaining in peace and loving them always, being sure that the Almighty's Goodness, which protects and envelops you, envelops and protects all of them too.

34

Spiritual Support

On behalf of beneficence, we share several resources, such as money, clothing, dwelling and foods. There is, however, a gift that we all need in the exchange of fraternity: the gift of encouragement.

We may think that those who stumble on the paths of extreme material shortage are the only people who lack forces. Nevertheless, in a matter of suffering, we very often surprise legions of fellows, in whose hearts hope is like a flame about to finish in the blow of adversity.

This man is very powerful in the financial field, but he carries the weight of terrible disappointments in his heart.

That one embellishes his name with competence and culture titles, but he brings the soul curved under displeasures and annoyances of every kind, as if he dragged hidden burdens.

Another one has got authority and influence in the orientation of a vast community, but he has his chest suffocated by pain, in the face of unknown sorrows that mark his hours.

That other shows himself as a model of healthiness in the shop windows of bodily health, yet, he carries with him a well of repressed tears, in view of the trials that burden his life.

Meditate on such realities and do not deny the gift of courage to any of your brothers and sisters along the way. If someone has failed, tell him about the new lessons that time brings us all;

If somebody has fallen, stretch out your arms to him with the renewing faith that set us again on the path of elevation.

If he went into despair, give him the blessing of peace, and if he has plunged into sadness, then offer him the message of good courage…

There is no one who can dispense with spiritual support

Right now, many of us need the courage to learn, serve, understand and wait… And probably later, when in more difficult moments of the human travel, we all will need the courage to bless and suffer, endure and live.

35

Your Possessions

You shall never condemn the possession or express any movement of extortion around it.

Consider the providence of God, who does not allow the sun above, or the air we breathe to be rationed, and you will understand that the Supreme Lord provides you the possession on condition of a sacred deposit, observing your capacity to help your neighbor.

This concession has such a deep meaning that there always comes a moment when the grantee has to transfer it to someone else's hands, in order to receive, in the Life Beyond, the fruits of credits or debits that he has achieved with it, before the Divine Accounting. Even so, you will not despise it. You shall use it as an instrument of goodness, with which you can build your own happiness, by bringing happiness to others.

You will take from it the support that the world owes you, without forgetting the support that you owe the world.

By using it, you will make possible the honest work that protects your fellows of life experience, the ennobling culture in favor of the school, the help to homes in trials and the relief to the brothers who suffer disease and scarcity.

Not only will you consider material resources as your property, in the framework of divine loans, but you will also bring to the harvest of love for the neighbor, the power, intelligence, authority, art, technique or the degrees you own, honoring the All-Merciful.

Your possession is, in essence, the possibility of your being helpful.

You shall organize with what you have and can, your gift of action and cooperation, in order that life is better, wherever you are, so suppressing the constraints of the need and intensifying the service of blessing.

Whenever the idea of scantiness suggests you the distance from good works, remember Jesus. He lived and acted in homes and borrowed boats, without owning even a stone to rest his head, and gave of himself the blessed gift of love, transforming it into an inalienable treasure of the world for the sustenance of God's Kingdom.

36

In Matters of Faith

You will keep the faith.

You will learn with it to sing praises for the blessings of the Supreme Father, expressing the gratitude that is born from your spirit. Nevertheless, above all, you will take it as a safe guide on the path of the regenerative trials on the Earth, in order to fulfill worthily the will of the Lord, in the accomplishment of the obligations that life reserved for you.

You will cultivate the faith.

You will find in it, basic resources that will endorse your requests addressed to the Divine Providence. However, you will devote yourself to use it as a sustainer of your strength, in the duty to be fulfilled, so you do not disappoint the Higher Plan in the cooperation that the Spiritual World asks from you in favor of your brothers.

You shall speak of faith.

You will keep its flare on your lips, giving rise to peace and security in those who hear you. Though, you will find in it your precious anchor, in order that you do not grow disheartened in the testimonies of abnegation that the world expects from you, trying to smile instead of crying, on days of suffering and ordeal, when the notes of enthusiasm often falter on your mouth.

You will respect the faith.

You will see in it the dominant trait of the great spirits that we worship, in the class of heroes and giants of virtue, transformed in beacons of light on the trails of humanity.

You shall realize, nevertheless, that it is also a treasure-trove of energies at your disposal, in the everyday experience, giving you the ability to achieve the miracles of love, starting from your inner life or the heart of your own home.

Paul of Tarsus stated that the human being will be saved by faith, but undoubtedly, he did not refer to sterile words and convictions. Certainly, the friend of the Gentiles meant that the human spirit will improve and regenerate using positive confidence in God and in oneself, in the construction of the general welfare.

Faith transubstantiated into good works, translated into service and raised to the high level of the teachings that it exposes, in the domains of the realization and activity. So true is the assertion in which the apostle showed faith as a dynamic resource, in the individual field, for the construction of the Divine Kingdom that he affirmed, compelling, in verse 22 of the 14th chapter of his Epistle to the Romans:

"Have you faith? Have it to yourself before God."

37

Peace of Mind

We have today, everywhere on Earth, an essential problem to solve: the conquest of peace of mind. In it are developed all the roots of the solution for the other problems that beset the soul.

However, what guidelines should we adopt to achieve it?

Should we use force, impose conditions, create circumstances?

We do not ignore that tension can only impede the flow of creative energies emanated from hidden areas of the spirit, aggravating conflicts and masking deep realities of our inner life, usually unmanifested.

The peace of mind, on the contrary, excludes the rashness and stress, to stop and consolidate it in serenity and understanding. For this reason, if we wish to obtain it, we urgently need to bring our syndromes of anxiety and anguish to the invisible providence that supports us.

The psychological sciences of today name this resource as "creative and active power of the unconscious", but simplifying concepts, in order to adapt them to the environment of our faith, we call it "the omniscient power of God in us".

As we surrender ourselves to God's plans, and trust Him with the intricate problems that arise in our daily life, we find the exact rule of the tranquility susceptible to assure us balance in the inner world for the ideal performance in life.

We should entrust to God the obscure part of our evolutionary journey, but without disregarding the duty that falls to us.

Working and waiting, doing the best we can.

Faith and service. Calm without idleness.

Let us think about it, and jettison the burden of destructive agents of hate, resentment, guilt, condemnation, criticism or bitterness that we usually drag in the mud of hostility, with which we treat life, so often ruining time and health, opportunity and interests.

Let us base our peace of mind on one simple conclusion: God, who has sustained us so far, will also sustain us from this moment onwards.

In short, let us remember the evangelical text, which wisely warns:

"If God is for us, who can be against us?"

38

Reactions

Before the fact that we will have to respond for our actions to the Laws of the Universe, it is imperative to realize that the occurrences that happen to us are not the most important things in our lives, but actually our reactions before them.

Through the circumstances, life writes the lessons we need. Consequently, in the succession of days, we are impelled to the testimonies of our learning of the values received on the phase of incarnation.

There are people, who make of the physical health a springboard for spiritual losses, and there are those who carry painful diseases in the body, but they transfigure them into precious instruments for the soul rehabilitation.

We see people who enjoy the benefits of immense material fortune, digging with them the pit of grief into which they throw themselves, and others who are stuck to heavy ties of penury, converting them into a pathway of access to prosperity.

Therefore, we understand that if there are similar individual reactions, we cannot see them, in any part, absolutely analogous with each other.

In view of this, consider, from time to time, your own path taken so far.

What do you do with the successes and failures that interest your personality? What do you do with the comfort?

How do you behave before the collaboration of friends and the hostility of enemies? In what do you convert what you are, what you have, get, know, and enjoy?

Let us meditate on it while the Superior Plans guarantee us the opportunity of sojourn on Earth, be it in the condition of incarnate or discarnate spirits. The supposed goods and evils of the world are the didactic material on which we appose the seal of our replicas, inducing the world about what it should do for us.

The Divine Scripture says: 'To each according to his deeds", which ultimately means that the response of human beings towards life is what will decide the fate of each.

39

You will Help for Love

You will help for the sake of love in the tasks of charity.

You will not be seduced by the fascinating verb of those who use the gold of the word to increase violence in the name of freedom, and those who lead you to believe that life is a burden of disillusionments.

You will adopt discipline as a standard of action in your environment of renovating work, and you will educate yourself according to the principles of the good, raising the level of your existence and sublimating the circumstances.

You will hear from many that it is useless to suffer to benefit others, and to sow for the sustenance of ingratitude; though, you will remember the anonymous benefactors that made your path smoother, putting out their lights so many times, so you could shine.

You will remember your childhood in the household refuge, and you will realize that you rose up, above all, from the goodness with which your heart was sheltered. You did not obtain the maternal tenderness with financial resources, and you did not pay your father for the residence on which he kept your boyhood. You also did not buy the affection of those who balanced your first steps, and did not pay for the tenderness of those who raised your thoughts in the light of prayer, teaching you to pronounce the name of God!

Consider the roots of love with which the All-Merciful has shaped the foundation of our lives, and collaborate wherever you are, in order that the good is the support of everyone.

You will see, in those around you, authentic brothers and sisters before the Divine Providence. You will help the less good to become good, and will support the good to become better.

If disturbance hinders your path, then serve, without ostentation, and the trail of liberation will be open to you, giving you access to the way forward.

If insults stone you, shield yourself in the well-done duty and serve always, being sure that goodness, with the strength of time, is the natural goal of all readjustments.

Many people command, require, or discuss…

You will be the one who serves; the Samaritan of the blessing; the understanding of the misunderstood, the light of those who struggle in the shadows; the courage of the sad, and the support of the ones who grieve in the rearguard!

So yet when you see yourself absolutely alone, in the ministry of the good, you will be faithful to the obligation to serve, bearing in mind that one day, an Angel in the form of a man, climbed an arid mount, in supreme abandonment, carrying the cross of his own sacrifice.

Though, because he served and served, forgiving and forgiving, he was, in the darkness of death the sun of the nations, in perpetuity of light and love to the whole world.

40

Our Problems

In general, as a problem arises, we soon feel afflicted.

We often try to circumvent it through a deliberate escape. On other occasions, before confronting it, we embrace discouragement or revolt. So, there goes the opportunity of promotion.

As eternal spirits, sometimes we lose successive reincarnations only by the fear of facing fair and necessary difficulties regarding our improvement.

Problems, however, constitute the price of evolution.

There is no knowledge without experience, and there is no experience without trials.

Such principles prevail in all the levels of Nature. The embryo of the seed has a fundamental problem: how can it traverse the wrapper that protects it, to build its own path towards the light? The caterpillar has another: where should it rest to form a cocoon and become a butterfly?

If it were not the challenges and exercises of the school, both the culture and the civilization would be solely remote ideas in the field of humanity.

Do not be afraid before the problems that visit you. They are natural resources of life, measuring your capacity of adaptability and growth.

You will never be sure if you have enough reserves of courage, without the obstacle that teaches you to decipher the secrets of self-overcoming, and neither would you know if you really have love, without the pain that teaches you to unlock the purest feelings of the heart.

Problems are synonyms of lessons. If your path is full of them, it means that you have attained the maturity of spirit, with the possibility to attend simultaneously various improvement courses in the school of the world.

Bless the opportunity to witness your abnegation and faith, once every moment of comprehending and forgiving, helping and edifying, is a chance to learn and time to progress.

41

Indication of Life

"A recipe that heals our sufferings; an indication to forget the evil" – many people ask.

Even so, it is imperative to recognize that the good is so vital and spontaneous on our common path, that we usually receive it without at least thinking about gratitude.

Example: the incessant and free cooperation of the sun and the air, which nourish us.

In general, we do not remember that we live immersed in the infinite ocean of the Father's Infinite Goodness.

On many occasions, instead of following the right moves of the currents of Universal Love, in which we exist and breathe, we fight against them, squandering in vain our own forces, with the only intention of solemnizing tiny waste sludge that passes by us, on the way to oblivion and disintegration.

If you find yourself with the real purpose of putting a barrier to evil influences, make a promise to yourself, to count the blessings around you, and those others that happen to you in the everyday life, such as: the shelter at home, the relative health, the remedy that supplements your energies, the bread, clothing, pure water, decent work, the resources that help the realization of commitments without problems of consciousness, the study as much as you want, the values of friendship, the possibilities to understand and to assist, the treasure of prayer, the constant support for an inner renewal, the encouraging words of someone...

Make every morning a list of the goods that the Almighty ever placed at your disposal, and you will see that the evil is a passing cloud in the sky of your ideas and emotions.

Then you will quickly extricate yourself from all the ties that maybe still bind you to the shadow of yesterday, to find today the best time to feel the good, know and believe in the good, and do good, on the evolving journey we all live, seeking step by step, the perfect life for the greater happiness.

42

Before the Fallen

It is so easy to abandon our fallen brothers… Many people pass by those who suffered in terrible mistakes and say nothing to console them, but phrases like these: "I warned you", "I told you so much"… In spite of this, only the Divine Justice can measure the struggles of resistance that lie behind the fall of our unfortunate friends.

This man was impelled to delinquency; people know him now by a Police record, but until his ruin was complete, how much abandonment and penury he has dragged in his life, perhaps since the most distant days of his childhood!

That other man threw himself into chasms of revolt and discouragement, embracing the drunkenness; however, until he had discredited himself, how many days and nights of woe he has undergone, writhing under the weight of temptation, in the attempt not to fall!

That woman came into the way of folly, and settled herself in the well of unhappiness that she dug for herself; though, in how many thorns of need and disruption she was wounded until the madness installed itself in her tormented brain!

Another man abandoned tasks and appointments, in whose implementation he had searched for the victory of his soul, and slipped into unworthy experiences, so harming the basis of his own existence. Nevertheless, how many tribulations he surely has experienced and how many tears he shed, until his reason darkened, paving the way for irresponsibility and dementia!!

Before the brothers and sisters pointed by censorship, never condemn! Think about the trails of ordeals and sadness that they must have walked until their feet faltered, feeble, during the difficult journey!! Reflect on the invisible currents of fire, which must have burnt their mind, until they gave in to the terrible compulsions of darkness...

Then, and only then will you feel the need to think about the good, to speak of the good, seek for the good and do solely the good, comprehending, finally, the loving statement of Jesus:

"It is not the healthy who need a doctor, but the sick."

43

Near You

You hear expressive communications from the Spiritual World about the work that awaits you in the world.

Usually, after that, you let your thoughts ramble in the distance, searching for news of the huge evils that plague the Earth.

You know the great needs claim major interventions, and you soon reflect on the gigantic missions, such as war termination, the abolition of racial prejudices, which undermine whole peoples, the cure of diseases that flog the Humanity or the deciphering of science riddles.

As a matter of fact, all this demand the presence of specialized missionaries; though, there is an urgent need for you to fulfill the Divine Will, by carrying out the less important duties that pile up beside you.

Maybe there is not so far any call asking you to serve in armed conflicts in other lands, but the Lord requests you to appease the hearts that surround you, in order that serenity and peace preside over the familiar environment.

For the time being, it is likely that no one expects from you any collaboration in a permanent banishment of diseases considered incurable; nevertheless, the Lord asks you for relief in favor of the sick brothers and sisters who mourn and suffer in your sphere of personal and direct influence.

Probably, you still do not have your word invited to outline guidelines ahead of the crowds. However, the Lord counts on your kind and understanding verb in your social sphere, ensuring peace and lifting in those who share life with you.

You do not know if you bring some incumbency from the High Plan to respond to challenges of Nature with a discovery of significant value to humanity. Nevertheless, it is sure that the Lord expects your contribution, to solve little problems, in the trials context of people who live together with you, in the daily routine.

Every service aiming at the good of others has great importance to the Divine Master.

It is fair, thus, to be interested in all the serious matters on the Planet, and you must do as much as you can, in favor of your brothers and sisters who are far from you. Even so, it is imperative to understand that the Lord awaits your determined cooperation in all tasks of love, comprehension, tolerance, fraternal support, and incessant service, for the benefit of all those who are near you.

44

Conversation in Family

Should you notice the moral failure of someone, do not tarry on the superficial analysis of things. Deepen yourself in the examination of the causes, so that the injustice does not stain your heart.

Let us remember that the doctor does not always find the illness by what he sees, but above all, by what he does not see, supported on the laboratory cooperation.

Rarely is all the evil, the evil we see on the visible side of circumstances. Humanity is composed of peoples; each nation is based on communities; each community is an aggregation of groups; each group is a constellation of souls.

Do not speak about any unfortunate event, without appreciating all the facts that gave rise to it.

How could we set the position of a wife, supposedly in helplessness, without considering the husband conduct, called by the principles of cause and effect to support her?

So how could we understand a man, tumbled in a passion crime, without analyzing the woman who took him to such folly? What should we think about the young boys and girls who have gone astray, without touching the adults who let them adrift?

How should we understand the penury of the elder, without considering the abandonment to which they were voted on by the younger? How could we blame solely the bad, without asking the good ones what they have done for them, in the realm of family interaction?

So how could we condemn uniquely the sinners, without knowing about what guidance they received from the righteous, with whom they share the everyday life? Are fair or insensitive the spirits called righteous, when they relegate their brothers and sisters to the errors of injustice, without any phrase to clear their reasoning?

Will they be correct or ungrateful, the spirits supposedly fair when they leave their brothers and sisters sunk in error, without the slightest support to redo their balance?

Brothers of each other by the ties of the great family, the Humanity, when we relate to our fallen fellows, before censuring them, we should ask ourselves what kind of benefit we have already made for them, so that they did not slip in the mud that disfigures their divine face of God's children, so needy of God's blessings as us.

Let us meditate on it, for once practicing such teachings, whenever we are impelled to check the behavior of someone, we will have the mercy as inspiration and support, lest we will fail to practice the imperative of love to the glory of the right.

45

Mutual Support

Despite the traveller condition that represents you in the world, from time to time, think of your heart as the place that other travellers may use for recovery or information, help or rest.

Jettison from the entrance of your inner house any pebbles susceptible to hurt the feet of those who seek you, and there turn on the light of compassion, with which you can help and understand everyone, according to each one's needs.

Recall the obstacles you have already surmounted, and do not allow that the shelter of your soul be converted in a maze of shadows for the people who search for you.

You know that life has enough charge of reality to clarify those who pass in the carriage of fallacy. Thus, do not throw in their face, the illusions with which they adorn themselves to meet reality. As you welcome those who carry visible deficiencies, cover them with the kindness of your look, without mentioning the wounds that temporarily disfigure their lives.

In spirit, all of us give shelter to one another. Concede the environment of peace and the table of blessing to the brothers that ask you for support. In short, be merciful to all those who pass by the refuge of your soul! Like us, which one will live without problems? Which one will move forward, without the pain purifying their vision?

Before good people, be merciful, once you are unaware of the number of thorns placed daily into their hearts, so they are faithful to the good. In the face of the bad, be doubly compassionate, for we do not ignore how much suffering awaits them along the way, in order that they disentangle from evil.

Whoever knocks at the gates of your appreciation, bless them with the word of comprehension; and if someone comes to be with you in the same sphere of work and ideal, in some short or long station of conviviality, give this person the best you can.

Do not feel, think, speak or do anything without the advice of compassion. We are all guests of each other, and if today somebody asks you for attention and zeal, protection and tenderness, in view of the distressing surprises on the path, maybe tomorrow other afflictive surprises also wait for you.

46

Moral Assistance

On many circumstances, we get afflicted due to the impossibility to change the thinking or the direction taken by beloved ones.

How could we help a son, who gets distant from us through attitudes we find undesirable, or support a friend, who insists on a path that does not seem the best?

Sometimes, the person in question is someone who deserved a long time of our convenience and tenderness; in other circumstances of life, it is someone who used to be a beacon of light for us.

Everything that was harmony goes into the domain of apparent contradictions, and all that seemed a triumphant task, gives us the impression of a lost work, going back to square one.

At this point of query and strangeness, it is imperative to understand that we all have a limited part of service and cooperation in the spiritual edification of each other, after which comes the part of God.

The farmer promotes favorable conditions to plant a crop, but he cannot place the embryo into the seed; he protects the tree, but he did not invent the sap.

So happens to us, on the lines of existence. Each of us can offer to the others only the collaboration in accordance with their capacity. Beyond it, there is an inner zone in everyone, where the Divine Providence works through unexpected processes, and often, downright inaccessible to our narrow comprehension.

Hence, before beloved ones that have complicated their paths, the best moral aid with which we can help them will be always the blessing of the silent prayer, so that they accept, wherever they are, the Divine Support that never fails.

Whatever is the problem presented by dear ones, let us keep our own serenity and fulfill the part of service and devotion that we owe them. After this, it is crucial to decide on giving them to the workshop of life, in whose gears and experiences they will reap, as much as we all have received, the hidden part of the love and assistance of God.

47

Offenses and Offenders

As soon as appear before us any problems of offense, disadvantage, discord or incomprehension, it is imperative to observe how the study of one's own reactions is important for the spirit, so that sorrow does not come in touch with the forces that dwell in the mind.

When we feel resentment, we cut on the tissues of our own soul, and we accommodate with the poison that others throw at us, giving shelter to unnecessary suffering, or attracting the presence of death. That's because, in the face of logic, all the disadvantages in the chapter of offenses weigh on those who take the initiative of evil.

The offender can be the one that is under regrettable obsessive processes; someone who carries hidden diseases; who acts under the impulse and makes tremendous mistakes, or crosses the cloud of the so-called "unfortunate moment". When it is not so, it is a person who brings the spiritual vision fogged by the dust of ignorance, which is a misfortune like any other in the world.

It still falls to the offender the nightmare of repentance, the personal heartbreak, the longing for invigoration, and the frustration compounded by the certainty of having injured oneself spiritually.

For the offended hearts, it remains only a danger - the danger of resentment, which, by the way, does not have the slightest meaning when we bring the conscience pacified in the accomplished duty.

Understanding this, never respond to evil with evil. Bear in mind that the offenders are almost always victims of obsessive processes, or confused, sick or frankly unhappy fellows, to whom we cannot attribute greater responsibilities, for the difficult conditions in which they live.

Jesus said: *"Love your enemies."*

This instruction, in our view, besides impelling us to the virtue of tolerance, makes us think that the offended should beware, using the armor of love and patience, lest suffer the blows of resentment, for the offenders already carry with them the fire of remorse and the gall of disapproval.

48

Trials and Prayers

We often refer to difficult circumstances as insurmountable hurdles, brought by the blind forces of fate, devastating our courage and joy of living, only because, on certain occasions, our supplications to the Lord do not obtain favorable and ready responses.

However, another will be our point of view, if we consider that the intelligent resources of life bring us critical events to check our capacity of self-overcoming.

Let us imagine the dismantling and disorder that they would lead to the world if all our wishes were immediately met. On the other hand, let us analyze the mutability of our situations and dispositions, and we will find, that much of the providence we have requested to the Almighty, frequently finds us on other trails of petition when granted.

Thus, the illicit character of our complaints, when claiming that the Lord does not always hear us on days of anguish.

Today we wish this or that, tomorrow we no longer want it.

We compete for the possession of a given object, and we lose interest in its concession, after obtaining it.

How could we expect that the Divine Mercy suppressed our help or medication, the relief or lesson, if difficult times are the necessary tools for our souls to be correctly worked for the tasks of the needed development?

If embarrassing trials reach you on the path, do not allow yourself the omission of the struggle, through escape or discouragement. Keep working on the area that they afflict you, being certain that they are factors of promotion, raising your level.

Tolerate the unfavorable conditions that emerge on the daily path, once if you accept them, serving and edifying, you shall soon notice that the Heaven support sustains you, in your crossing all of them, for in no place, and in no time, are we separated from God.

49

Giving and Doing

If you leave your heart in what you give and do, then nobody will be able to foresee the granaries of blessings that will come from such attitude.

You will solve the problems of the fellow in material difficulties; nevertheless, if you embrace him as a true brother, you will help him to untangle the spirit of the ideas of scarcity and inertia, urging him to work in a decent job. From this point of recovery, he will go ahead with your blessing of fraternity, and no one will imagine the fruits of growth and joy that others will gather from your initial cooperation.

You will visit the patient, thrilling him with your proof of appreciation; however, if you welcome him within yourself, in the condition of a dear one, you will liberate him from the thoughts of desolation and abandonment, restoring the peace of his soul. From this condition of readjustment, he will go ahead, and even when he is still stricken with a difficult disease, you will not be able to calculate the rewards of patience and compliance that others will receive from your affective gesture.

If you only pay the wages stipulated in the contract to the employee who serves you, giving money to his hands and dryness to his heart, you may briefly have a potential opponent of your work.

In the school, if you circumscribe yourself to the established program, ministering the class scheduled to the students, without enriching it with kindness and understanding, it is probable that you will be shortly followed by a whole class consisting of rebellious and repeating students.

We do not mention this for you to act irresponsibly. We wish to stress that if we want to help and build, at the same time, then it is necessary to set our own soul in that what we grant and accomplish.

In short, everything you give and do is important as an aid to your neighbor, but it is always more important to others and to yourself, the way you give this or do that, as all the benefit without love is compared to the shallow well, whose yesterday's waters dry today for lack of life and movement.

50

How to Forgive

In most cases, the imperative of forgiveness arises between our friends and us, when the sweet juice of confidence sours in our hearts.

This happens because, generally, the deepest sorrows emerge among the spirits bound to each other, in the wake of social interaction.

When our relationships become sick, in the interchange with certain friends, who, according to our opinion, transfigure into our opponents, let us ask ourselves honestly: "how should I forgive, if forgiving is not limited to a matter of lips, but a problem that affects the innermost mechanisms of feelings?"

That done, we should recognize that:

- The people in mistake belong to God and not to us;
- We also have errors to correct and adjustments in development;
- It is not fair the attempt to keep them in our points of view, when they are, just like it happens to us, under the will of the Divine Wisdom, which better befits to each one, on the path of betterment and progress.

Then, let us remember the blessings with which such people have enriched us in the past, and let us keep our feeling of gratitude for them, as life prescribes for us.

Let us also remember that God has already given them new opportunities for action and elevation, in other sectors of service and that it will not be reasonable on our part to keep complaints against them at the tribunal of life, when the Almighty does not neglect them love and confidence.

When you truly trust yourself to God, to God trusting your adversaries as your authentic brothers and sisters, as needed of the Divine Support as yourself, you will penetrate the true meaning of Christ's words: *"Forgive us our debts as we forgive our debtors"*, reconciling to life and to your own soul. Then you will be able to kiss again the face of him, who has offended you, and whoever did it will find God with you, and they will tell you with the purest joy of the heart: "Blessed are you!"

51

We are not Exceptions

When you suffer pinpricks in the world, do not allow yourself to fall in the labyrinth of great complications for it.

It is inevitable that the smallest crack in the car receives immediate repairs, if the traveller does not want to risk.

In body impairments, you should use remedies, gymnastics, diets, and surgeries, and in the soul evils, you will not cure yourself only with expectation. It is urgent to employ observations, decisions, rules and studies.

When anxiety or distress visits you, analyze yourself; deliberate about what you should do to avoid imbalance and disorder; take responsibility for your own discipline and inspect the field of action where you move.

Without a doubt, you need redoing and comfort; despite this, in favor of your own betterment, learn to recognize that, when it comes to suffering, you are no exception.

Reflect on those who carry burdens heavier than yours. Those who want to walk as naturally as you walk, and remain fastened on motionless beds; those who yearn to see as you do, and grope in the shade; the ones who see your abundant table, without resources to enjoy it. Also, those people who would be relieved to share your inner security, and have the head burning by invisible flames of obsession.

Gaze at the vanguard of those that have become higher, so you encourage yourself to the spiritual ascent; though, do not forget to look at the rearguard, in order to comfort yourself with the already conquered values, which you can distribute clearly for the benefit of others.

Suffer, by learning, and elevate yourself, by helping. This is the program of life's school itself, inasmuch as be it in the ascension or in the rescue, improving or repairing errors, the law of trials is the sealer agent of the worthiness of each one, and it does not create privilege or favor, clandestinity or exception for anyone.

52

Opponents

Without a doubt, if we respect the skills and commitments of the neighbor, why should we underestimate their opinions?

In general, we want from the others the perfect qualities that we do not own yet, and on this basis, it is natural that the opponents give us warnings, and point us directions to mend our ways or to fight us.

If our opponents were only those who have never enjoyed our conviviality, and solely antagonized us due to their points of view, it would be easy to ignore or to forget them. Nevertheless, they are also, and plenty of times, those same fellows of ideal, who vibrated with us in the same house, who ensured us confidence and tenderness, or flew for us the flag of hope and peace.

Superficially modified by the circumstances of life, they frequently no longer share our goals and desires, and if they emit opinions around the activities in which they left us, they often seem contrary to our purposes, whose fulfillment gives us peace and balance, encouragement and joy.

When this happens, we should have respect for them the necessary respect. What we see from a given point of the path does not always keep the same characteristics, if we exchange positions.

The opinions of others are properties of others, claiming our consideration. If they bring applicable reproaches, let us know how we should receive them, taking their value in the correction that becomes necessary.

If they bring disapprovals, let us respond with blessings; if they contain untruths, let us be merciful towards those who pronounce them, and if they demand from us, attitudes and changes incompatible with our conscience, let us remain faithful to the duties we have embraced before the Lord. We will formulate votes so that they - our opponents and brothers of the heart - when brought to our position, can efficiently carry out all the good we were not able to do.

53

Arguments

Time of annoyance or displeasure: time of silence and prayer. Clarify, analyze, notice, observe, but every time that bitterness appears, even if from afar, leave the conversation or the understanding for later.

Discussing, in the sense of arguing or quarreling is the same as throwing kerosene on the bonfire.

Whenever we become irritated, we immediately connect our thoughts to areas of shadow or disturbance. Then, the word is debited to the account of repentance, once we easily exaggerate impressions, embrace false judgments, provoke negative reactions, or hurt someone unintentionally.

Worst of all: the ruptures in the harmonious relationships at home or in fraternal groups begin from trifles, like tiny loopholes, by which vigorous dams fall in, giving rise to the calamities of floods.

Let us tolerate setbacks and annoyances of life, moving them away from daily life, just like who cleans a minefield.

Let us accept the claims of others, pay for the loss that is possible to rescue without great sacrifice, and forget the thoughtless phrase, or the gesture of disregard, often involuntary, with which someone has wounded us.

Never value unpleasant events or frivolities intended to blacken your optimism. Some say that the discussion brings to light. Perhaps, it is frequently a factor of discernment, when managed by high spirits; even so, in many other cases, it does nothing more than supporting discord and turning off the light.

54

In the Sublime Initiation

When Jesus called us to perfection, he clearly knew the burden of faults and deficiencies that made our account still negative before the Accounting of Life.

Thus, it is urgent to comprehend the meaning of such invitation, accepting, on our part, the sublime initiation.

In the rough rise, in the search for the eternal values, the Laws of the Universe do not request from us any blazon of spiritual greatness. Beings in a laborious march on the evolutionary path, let us, therefore, dedicate ourselves to the foundations of the apprenticeship.

In times of crisis, the Divine Statutes do not ask from us certificates of superiority, radiating indifference, but they wish our suffering it with reflection and dignity, assimilating the advice of experience.

When coping with invectives and jeers, the Instructions of the Lord, do not require from us the mask of impassivity, but they want us to overcome them bravely, assimilating their passage with the blessing of fraternal comprehension.

Faced with temptations, life does not expect that we stand before them under anesthesia, but that we neutralize them with patience and courage, amassing the lessons they bring in our own favor.

Challenged by the worst disillusionments, the Regulations of Eternity do not ask from us any testimony of moral aridity, but they wish that we strive to forget such grief, without the slightest expression of discouragement, embracing greater demonstrations of service.

Let us refrain from adorning life with implausible expectations. We are human creatures, on the way to the necessary sublimation and, on this condition, to make mistakes and correct ourselves in order to succeed more and more, are imperatives of our route.

Despite this, we should remain convinced, since today, that if by now it is impossible for us to wear the tunic of the angels, we can and must enroll in the school of the good spirits.

55

Our Share

Maybe you do not notice it. Even so, each day you add something yours to the field of life.

The fields of the duties that you have embraced are those places where you leave your mark, necessarily; but you have other domains of work and time, in which the Lord allows you to act freely, so as to impregnate them with the signs of your passage.

Analyze by yourself the situations with which you are faced, hour to hour. By all the flanks, requests and demands come: tasks, commitments, contacts, news, events, comments, information, rumors. Whether you want it or not, your share of influence counts in the overall sum of decisions and achievements of the community, for in matters of expression, even your silence counts.

We do not mean it, for you to wake up, each day, in an alarmist position. We say it, so that the circumstances, whatever they are, find us with open soul to the patronage and expansion of the good.

Let us be accustomed to serving and blessing effortlessly, as much as we take possession of the air, breathing mechanically. Let us have the habit to understand and help others without the idea of sacrifice.

We learn and teach charity in all the subjects of the human need.

Let us make it the spiritual bread of life.

Believe it or not, everything we feel, think, say or accomplish, defines our daily contribution, in the amount of happy or less happy forces and possibilities of existence.

Let us meditate on it. Let us reflect on the share of influence and action that we impose to life, in the person of our neighbor, once everything we give to life, life will also bring to us.

56

God Shall Come

Do not be discouraged under the burden of ordeals, nor lose heart in the mist of tears.

In the most difficult times, remember that God shall come to help us.

You will hear about the resounding triumphs of evil, inviting you to stop any effort in favor of good, under the pretext that the evil is supported by the huge legions of those who obtain its superficial advantages. Do not discuss. You will serve constantly the general well-being, being sure that God shall come by the pathways of time, to restore the good ones to their fair place.

You will see those who make you feel that the disagreements of the world are not consistent with the work of peace, with the excuse that the human needs the war as an imperative of evolution. Do not discuss. You will give all the support to the sustenance of concord, wherever you are, aware that God shall come, by the pathways of time, to establish the perfect solidarity among Nations.

You will hear long dissertations on the deterioration of manners, leading you to disbelieve the social dignity. Do not discuss. You will respect yourself, and will not abandon the righteously done duty, in the belief that God shall come, by the pathways of time, to reset the convulsed sectors of the human community, placing again each of them on their right path.

Frequently, on your own personal path, bitter predictions will search for you, on the part of many fellows, trying to fasten your mental field on the most scabrous issues of the daily life…

We will hear worrying allusions around the commitments we have embraced; about people, we are fond of, and institutions that we have offered the best of our aspirations for the higher life…

Let us respect all the informant friends who request our attention to the impact of evil, and, as much as possible, let us cooperate with them in its extinction. Nevertheless, let us keep the heart invariably in the luminous tunic of hope, by praying and working, watching and serving, convinced that God, Whose infinite goodness sustained us yesterday and today, will also sustain us tomorrow.

Whatever the challenges and distresses of the path, never be overcome by the force of darkness, and make shine in your own heart the inarticulate message of eternal love, that the light of the open skies gives you, every morning, from horizon to horizon:

"God shall come."

57

The Best Happens

Surrender to God: the right attitude for victory in life.

This surrender, however, does not mean the withdrawal of action or spiritual inertia.

First, the duty righteously fulfilled, and then, the acceptance. On this basis, we will recognize that circumstances bring us the best that life can offer. In the mechanism of happenings, the prayer or wish express the request.

Subsequent events consubstantiate the answer of life, and he who accomplishes the obligations that life brings to him, keeps the conscience safe and enabled, be it to the understanding or resignation.

In the spirit harmonized with the implementation of its own commitments, there is no place for despair. If any pain appears, it is taken as the lesser evil, frustrating pending disasters.

Unexpected problems express necessary delays on serious subjects, whose immediate solution would generate even more disturbing conflicts than the current ones. Supposed ingratitude emerges on the affective ground, just like a pruning of the existence's tree, favoring the higher production of peace and joy.

Even the natural death, when it visits the material home, sometimes misunderstood, is a blessed providence, avoiding personal and household torments, or restraining tragic events with unpredictable results.

Before the difficulties of daily life, let us silent any revolt impulses and thoughtless reactions, when faced with the hurdles of the path.

God responds right.

Let us fulfill the work that circumstances present to us, and after the accomplished responsibility, let us accept whatever comes, being certain that, for a clear conscience, the best happens.

58

Service to those who Serve

Beneficence little remembered: the one we owe to those who benefit us.

How many prodigies of love we can do, only by controlling states of impatience or anguish!

Inside your home, consider the importance of your smile to the maternal angel who overworks to help you, and the worth of your tranquility to the paternal heart, who would give everything to see you happy!

In your workgroup, remember the value of your peace in favor of your teammates, so they work with efficiency and harmony on the gears of action.

In the good works, think about the imperative of your attitudes of solidarity and comprehension, in the assistance to the brothers called to serious missions, in the direction or subalternity, in order to ensure the good works.

In many instances, from a simple phrase of affection, fountains of joy gush for many people.

Thus, even in the dark hours of sickness and prostration, think of the high meaning of your serenity to support the beloved ones around you.

Aid the physician who aids you, by offering him environment for the needed treatment. Facilitate the work of the nurses who assist you, so that they treat you with safety, without useless bustle.

We all have problems to solve, but we are all incited by the wisdom of life to give calmness and cooperation, peace and happiness to others, in order that they help us to solve our own problems.

We all need something; even so, it is indispensable to agree that we must give to receive.

In synthesis, there is nobody who does not have the necessity of someone's service; despite this, it is crucial to help and serve those who serve us, so they can more fully understand and help us.

59

About Virtue

If someone has an enormous fortune and might overdo lavishness or avarice, but strives to employ it in the welfare and progress, education and enlightenment of his neighbor…

If he has authority, with resources to handle his influence in his sole advantage, but uses it to help others…

If he is accused of being guilty, with elements to do justice in the manner he deems better, and prefers to forget the offense received, recognizing himself as also liable to err...

If he has already made all the services within his reach in favor of somebody, receiving invariably incomprehension as reply, and keeps assisting this individual, through the possible means, without claim or complaint…

⁓

This person will be placed, obviously, on a prominent place about the worst temptations that hounded him in life.

All of us, the spirits in evolution and redemption on the trails of the Universe, review the experiences in which we have failed. In view of this, all the trials of the Earth's school take the way of indispensable tests and teachings.

Some people reincarnate showing extreme physical beauty, in order to overcome permissiveness inclinations; others show a privileged brain to win the vanity of intelligence.

Others come back to Earth holding a valuable academic degree, in order to subjugate the propensity for abuse; alternatively, some fulfill difficult duties in the noble causes, to extinguish the impulses of defection or disloyalty.

~

All of us, in the boarding school of reincarnation, are examined in the lower tendencies we bring from past lives, in order to learn that we will only reach the good by overcoming the evil that searches for us, so many times as needed, even beyond the paid debit or the extinct shadow.

It is easy to see, therefore, that without the presence of temptation, the virtue does not appear, and so will always be, so that innocence is not a sterile flower, and the major theories of spiritual elevation are not frustrated seeds in the field of Humanity.

60

Trust in God

Never lose hope, even when in the worst conditions. Never condemn someone who has gotten embarrassed in the labyrinth of ordeal.

The roughest moment of a problem may be the one in which we find its solution. In many cases, the person you think most objectionable, in a serious offence, might often be the one that less guilt carries in the weft of evil that the shadows have woven.

Surely there will be a correction for the mistakes in darkness, by the mechanisms of order, as much as there will be a remedy for the sick by the medicine resources.

See, however, the merciful power of God, in the smallest sectors of nature. The smothered seed is the one that will sustain your granary. The stone placed on discipline is the agent that ensures you a firm construction.

Sorrows and tears are processes of life, in which you gain energies to go ahead, in the discharge of commitments embraced, so that your eyes get illuminated, in the accurate discernment.

On the hard days, stand up for life, raise your head, embrace the duties that events have given you, and bless the existence in which the Divine Providence has placed you.

No matter how deep is the pain that visits you; the blow which hurts you, the tribulation that seeks for you, or the suffering that weighs on your shoulders; do not be discouraged in faith, and keep faithful to your obligations, for if all the good seems lost, before the task in which you find yourself, be sure that God is with you, working on the other side.

Made in the USA
Middletown, DE
18 July 2017